50 THINGS TO DO AT THE BEACH

Published by
Princeton Architectural Press
202 Warren Street
Hudson, New York 12534
www.papress.com

Published in agreement with
Pavilion Books Company Ltd.
43 Great Ormond Street
London WC1N 3HZ

For Princeton Architectural Press:
Editor: Stephanie Holstein
Cover Design: Paul Wagner

Library of Congress Control Number:
2020948792

IMPORTANT SAFETY NOTICE
This book includes activities and projects that inherently
include the risk of injury or damage. We cannot guarantee
that following the activities or projects in this book
is safe for everyone. For this reason, this book is sold
without warranties or guarantees of any kind, expressed
or implied, and the publisher and the author disclaim
any liability for injuries, losses, and damages caused in
any way by the content of this book. The publisher and
author urge the reader to thoroughly review each activity
and to understand the use of all tools before beginning
any project. Always check that you have permission to
use the land where the activities or projects take place.
Children should always be supervised when undertaking
any activity or project in this book.

MIX
Paper from
responsible sources
FSC® C016973

50 THINGS
TO DO AT
THE BEACH

Easkey Britton

Illustrated by Maria Nilsson

PRINCETON ARCHITECTURAL PRESS · NEW YORK

Contents

Our Sea Connection

For many, the *ocean* remains an expanse of "blue space." What lies below the surface most humans may never see or experience first-hand. And yet, as you will learn in this book, our ocean and coasts affect us—even those of us who don't live nearby.

For me, I had the good fortune of a childhood spent in close proximity to the coast, full of the wonder of tidal movements, the power of the *sea*, and fast-moving weather fronts. At a very early age, I learned about intertidal zones from time spent in rock pools before following my mother and father into the surf. As a surfer I've learned that how I surf must honor the natural processes, flows, constraints, and rhythms of the ocean that are beyond human control.

From this book, I hope you will learn to reconnect with your oceanic roots during those special moments spent by the sea, and better understand how learning about the ocean and all that it does for us can influence our daily actions.

Our Watery Evolution: The Origins of Life

The sea is the great mother, supporting all life on Earth. Most of the water in the ocean today was formed four billion years ago. This ancient sea is also where the first life on Earth began. It remains in the salt water of our blood, our cells, and our DNA from when the first animals came ashore to live on land around one billion years ago. In the words of environmentalist Rachel Carson, these animals "carried with them a part of the sea in their bodies, a heritage which they passed on to their children and which even today links each land animal with its origin in the ancient sea." We are all connected to this watery origin in the ancient sea. Even today, our life begins swimming in our mother's womb. The water of the womb, called amniotic fluid, is actually the same density as seawater!

Ocean Literacy

Ocean literacy is defined as an understanding of the ocean's influence on you and your influence on the ocean. To be ocean-literate means to understand how and why we are connected to the ocean.

The story of our planet is the story of a watery sphere, enveloped in canals, rivers, springs, and streams that eventually flow to the ocean.

According to Dan Burgess of Wild Labs, this story of our blue planet seems "strangely muted and invisible in our modern culture where we have concreted over, digitally diverted, and put the ocean out of sight and therefore out of mind."

Stories about the ocean can help us make sense of the world and our place within it, while also sparking a curiosity that can create new ways of thinking about the ocean and our relationship with it.

Creating a more ocean-literate society means we are able to make informed and responsible decisions about the ocean and all the wonders it has to offer.

Oceans and Human Health

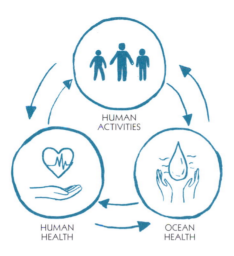

HUMAN
ACTIVITIES

HUMAN
HEALTH

OCEAN
HEALTH

The ocean does so much for us—
regulating our climate and providing us
with food, water, and the air we breathe.
Our health is intrinsically connected to
the ocean. Exploring this extraordinary
relationship is the basis for an emerging
scientific discipline called Oceans and
Human Health (OHH).

There is growing interest across
science, policy, and practice in the
ocean's impact on our health and
well-being. Scientists are just beginning
to discover how engaging with healthy
marine and coastal environments,
or *blue space*, can directly support
and restore health and well-being.

Time spent by the ocean is linked to
improved health, including feeling
happier, more energetic, and less
anxious.

However, there are also risks and
dangers that need to be understood,
such as storms (p. 36) and hazardous
rip currents (p. 24), as well as
sea pollution caused by human activity
which negatively affects our health.

OHH presents an opportunity to
understand our relationship with
the ocean in a new way, holistically
addressing complex challenges and
humanizing environmental crises.

Sick Sea: Pollution, Ocean Warming, and Other Harmful Impacts

As a lifelong surfer, I have an intimate connection with the ocean. What is of deep concern for me is the deterioration of our relationship with the natural world, especially the loss of our emotional connection with the ocean in all its wonder and aliveness. Our desire to be cleansed, to wash away the stress and worries that we carry on land, has become tainted in an ocean that is also becoming saturated with our waste.

Despite the vast size of the world's oceans—covering 70 percent of the planet and reaching almost seven miles (11 km) at its deepest point—there is no part of the ocean that remains unaffected by the growing and interconnected pressures of climate change, *biodiversity* loss, and further degradation caused by human activities, such as overfishing, seabed mining, shipping, and greenhouse gas emissions. Raw sewage pollution increases the risk of infections for bathers and water users, while poor water quality can lead to toxic algal blooms. Marine litter is another huge issue, with over 80 percent of all land waste ending up in the ocean and microplastics ending up in the marine food chain.

All of this reinforces the interdependent nature of our relationship with the ocean. This is what underpins my work as a marine social scientist—to better our understanding of our relationship with the ocean, and how this connection might be healed and restored.

Celebrating a Diverse and Inclusive Ocean

In my research exploring the links between oceans and human health, I've discovered how beneficial it is to be able to access the coast and sea. And yet, not all people have equal access to the ocean.

The ability to access and experience the sea may be shaped and limited by various aspects of our identity, such as gender (including non-binary), sexuality, race, ethnicity, and ability. The systemic marginalization of minority groups (including people marginalized by racism, sexism, or ableism) can be perpetuated in media reporting of water-based activities, like swimming and surfing, which can lead to their exclusion at beaches or surf breaks.

Universal access to watersports like surfing is being increasingly encouraged and supported. Globally, adaptive surfing events and competitions have grown, showing people living with disabilities that it is possible to experience the simple joy of catching a wave. Surfing is also being successfully used to help treat mental illness. The Naval Medical Center in San Diego introduces the sport to active duty military and veterans to help them alleviate symptoms of post-

traumatic syndrome such as depression and insomnia.

To restore the ocean as a supportive and inclusive place, we need to create spaces where the illusion of separation can crumble. In 2020 on World Ocean Day, as part of the Black Lives Matter movement and in the wake of the murder of George Floyd, Black Girls Surf, a group founded to support young girls and women of the diaspora in surfing, organized "paddle outs" in the United States and around the world. A paddle out is part of a Hawaiian tradition to celebrate a life and mourn its passing. The event, "Solidarity in Surfing," was a peaceful protest, honoring the Black lives lost to police brutality and denouncing racism in the United States and around the globe. In the words of Black Girls Surf founder Rhonda Harper: "Unity is the only way to make a real change."

Sea Sisters:
Empowering
Women and Girls

The United Nations Educational, Scientific and Cultural Organization (UNESCO) defines gender equality as "the equal valuing by society of the similarities and the differences of men and women, and the roles they play." Concerted global action to empower women and girls is still needed in order to achieve gender equality in all ocean-related sectors. These inequalities are even more pronounced for Black women, women from ethnic minorities, and women of developing nations.

Women are more likely to be affected by rapid environmental and climate change, which can be particularly acute in coastal regions. Four times as many women as men died in the Indian Ocean earthquake and tsunami in December 2004 as many women in the affected areas could not swim. In response, women are spearheading efforts to develop compassionate solutions around the world, turning the tide on gender inequality.

In Sri Lanka, despite it being a popular surfing destination, there is a prevalent stereotype that "Sri Lankan women don't surf." New organizations are helping to challenge that, such as the first all-female surf club, Arugam Bay Girls Surf Club, officially established in 2018, and the Sea Sisters initiative.

Sea Sisters is a swim and surf program which seeks to equip Sri Lankan women and girls with essential water-based life skills so they may see the ocean as a safe and enjoyable space. Surfing and swimming are helping facilitate social change by creating a safe space for local women and girls to enjoy the ocean and influence gender norms in Sri Lanka. Sea Sisters believes in an ocean community that celebrates diversity and equal opportunity for women and men.

"When I'm in the ocean, I feel free. I forget about everything. It's just me and the waves."
Sanu, Sea Sisters team member

By discovering this positive connection with the sea, local women and girls learn about the ocean and become its ambassadors—spreading awareness of environmental challenges and fostering more sustainable practices in their communities.

Sea Sisters also supports and provides funding for local female-led social enterprises that in turn help support their program. They call this "double empowerment," creating both jobs and opportunities to swim and surf!

Love Your Sea

Despite how interconnected our health is with the health of the ocean, there is a strong yet artificial divide between society and sea. We live increasingly urban and sedentary lives, removed from the lively natural world. This emotional disconnect from nature has serious consequences for our health, as well as the health of our blue planet. To restore our connection, we need new stories and experiences that celebrate how and why the ocean matters.

We are visitors of the sea, home to so much amazing life. Nearly 230,000 marine species have been discovered worldwide, from microscopic algae to gigantic blue whales, although many more are still to be discovered. Together, these species form important ecosystems that help support the healthy functioning of our planet; provide us with food, water and oxygen; regulate the weather; and protect us from the worst effects of storms and climate change. We must give all sea life the same care and respect we would give as a guest in someone's home.

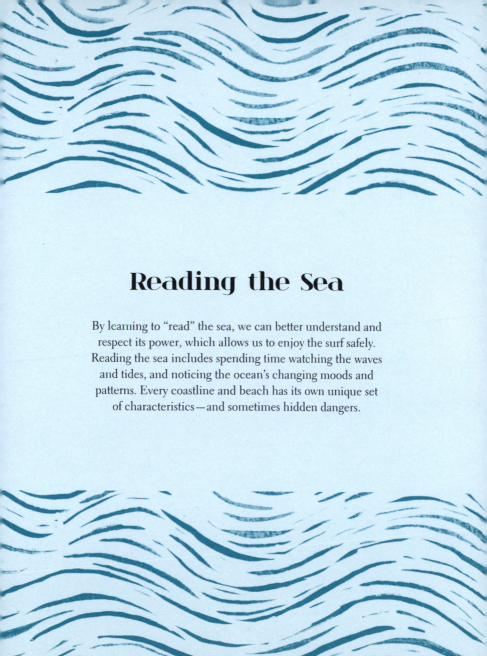

Reading the Sea

By learning to "read" the sea, we can better understand and respect its power, which allows us to enjoy the surf safely. Reading the sea includes spending time watching the waves and tides, and noticing the ocean's changing moods and patterns. Every coastline and beach has its own unique set of characteristics—and sometimes hidden dangers.

1

Watch the Waves

Waves are shaped by the wind. Their complex beauty is a wonderful reminder of how the unseen forces of nature work. The friction between storm-driven winds and the surface of the ocean creates a buildup of energy that begins to ripple outward and deepens into swells. This energy marches across the sea until meeting a continental shelf and shallow coastal waters.

Waves are not moving water. As waves of energy move through the water, water molecules spin in place without traveling with the wave. The underwater depth of the seabed, otherwise known as bathymetry, shapes this energy into breaking waves as they approach the coast, causing them to rise, steepen, curl, peel, and crash onto the shore.

Types of Breaking Waves

No two waves are the same. There are, however,
certain characteristics that some waves share.
The shape of these types of waves can change constantly
depending on tide, wind direction, and sand movement.

Surging waves are found on very steep
sloping beaches and rush up onto the
shore without losing much energy
in the beach layer known as "swash."
Some of this energy then moves back
to the sea and is called "backwash."

Spilling waves are found on beaches
with more gradual slopes. The crest of
the wave spills down the wave face.

Plunging waves are found where there
is a more abrupt transition from deep
to shallow waters. As the wave energy
below the surface slows, the wave face
becomes concave or hollow as the
crest pitches forward, creating what
surfers call a "tube."

Next time you go to the beach, see what kinds of waves you
can identify. Do you notice if the types of waves change
depending on the time of day or weather conditions (e.g.,
windy or calm, bigger or smaller swell, high or low tide)?

2

Move with the Tides

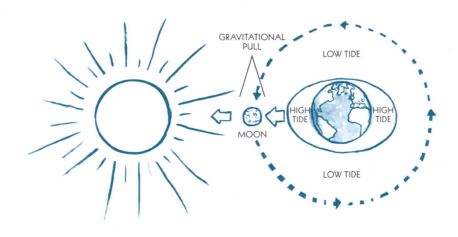

"Neither you nor I, with our earth-bound senses, know the foam and surge of the tide that beats over the crab hiding under the seaweed of his tide-pool home…"
Rachel Carson, "Undersea"

Tides are the daily ebb and flow of the ocean moving in and out from the shore. As the tide ebbs, we are provided a momentary glimpse of what lies beneath the sea—rock pools, intertidal seaweeds, and other hidden species—before these treasures are covered once again as the tide flows back in.

High tides and low tides are caused by the Moon. The Moon's gravitational pull on Earth creates a tidal force which causes the ocean to "bulge out" at the points closest to and farthest from the Moon. This "bulge" is high tide, when the sea level is at its highest point. These high tides on opposite ends of the Earth pull the water away from the rest of the ocean, causing a low tide on the remaining coastlines, when the sea level is at its lowest point.

The Earth's rotation causes the ocean to rise and fall twice a day along the world's many coasts, as if the ocean is slowly inhaling and exhaling. And it's not just the ocean that responds to the pull of the Moon, all bodies of water do—lakes, a cup of water, even our own bodies—but the movement is so small we hardly notice.

The Sun's gravity also influences tidal movements. The biggest tides of the year occur every two weeks, when the Sun, Moon, and Earth are in alignment and there's a new or full moon. At this time, the gravitational pull is at its strongest, creating "spring tides" with very high and very low tides. In between the new and full moons, the gravitational force of the Sun acts against that of the Moon, causing a small movement of tides called "neap tides."

It is important to understand the tidal behavior of your local area when you visit the ocean or coast so you don't get caught out by an incoming tide. A tide table for your local area can be very helpful.

To better understand the movement of tides—while documenting the passage of time in a fun way—go to the beach at low tide and place markers (stones or sticks) at regular intervals from the low tide line (where the sea meets the sand), to the high tide line (where you see a line of seaweed, driftwood, and other debris washed up from the previous high tide). Time how long it takes for the tide to reach each marker.

3

Understand Rip Currents

To enjoy your time safely by the ocean, it is very important to understand how rip currents work, how to spot them, and what to do if you get caught in one.

What is a Rip Current?

Rip currents are powerful channels of fast-moving water close to the shore that flow out to sea, like invisible rivers within the ocean.

There are many different types of rip currents caused by different forces at play in the sea, though breaking waves is a key ingredient. As waves break one after the other onto the shore, water piles up and follows the path of least resistance in order to return to the ocean, sometimes forming a rip current in the process. Rip currents are often formed where there's a channel in the beach, or a break in the *sandbar* a short distance from the shoreline. Strong currents can also appear along hard structures like piers, jetties, or sea cliffs.

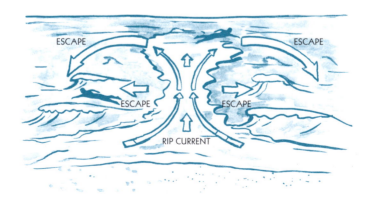

Some beaches don't have any rip currents, and on other beaches rip currents may come and go, but the risk is increased when there are bigger waves breaking, a steeply sloping beach, or bigger tides.

How Do You Spot a Rip Current?

It can be easier to spot a rip current if you are able to view the ocean from a higher vantage point. The key things to look for are: deeper, dark-colored water where there are fewer breaking waves; a rippled surface surrounded by smooth waters; anything floating out to sea; and foamy, discolored, or sandy water beyond the waves. Not all rips will have these features or are easy to spot, so it is always best to ask a lifeguard on duty or someone with local knowledge before venturing into the ocean.

What to Do If You Get Caught in a Rip Current

Keep calm. Never swim against the current; it is too powerful and will quickly exhaust you. Most rips are less than 100 ft (30 m) wide, so it is possible to swim out of the current in either direction parallel to the shoreline. If you cannot swim out of the rip, float on your back and go with the current until you are beyond its pull, usually 33–330 ft (10–100 m) from shore. If you are still unable to reach shore, draw attention to yourself—face the shore, wave your arms, and shout for help. See the next page for essential safety advice.

4

Know Your Beach, Know Your Limits

Being by the ocean is a wonderful experience that can both
energize and calm us. However, there are hazards to watch
out for in order to stay safe. Remember, the more you improve
your ocean literacy, the safer and more confident you will feel
by the sea.

Make Friends with the Sea

It is incredibly important to learn as much as you can about local conditions before visiting the coast, such as the water temperature, tide schedule, weather forecast, and the presence of rip currents. Never enter the water at an unfamiliar spot without consulting a lifeguard or someone with local knowledge, such as a surf instructor. Know your ability, never swim alone or beyond your depth, and take care to avoid rip currents (see page 24).

Cold Water Shock and the Gasp Reflex

Any water below 59°F (15°C) is defined as cold water and can seriously affect your breathing and movement. Sudden exposure to cold water results in the gasp reflex, causing you to inhale sharply. This can be followed by uncontrollable rapid breathing, or hyperventilation. Gradual immersion for short periods can help build up a healthy tolerance to cold water over time. Splash your face with water first before jumping in, breathe slowly, and the initial effects of cold water will pass in less than a minute.

Sun Exposure

The Sun's strong UV rays cause sunburn, even on cloudy days. To protect yourself, wear sunglasses and a sun hat; use sunscreen with a high sun protection factor (SPF) that is "reef-safe" (see page 132); and keep hydrated with lots of water to avoid heat exhaustion.

What the Sea Does for Us

The ocean is the source of all life on Earth. It impacts and benefits every person on the planet, even those who have never seen the sea. From the air we breathe, to the water we drink and use to grow our food, to regulating weather patterns and creating a buffer against the effects of climate change, the sea has a positive impact on our health and well-being in so many ways.

5

Understand Our Life Support System

The ocean is our life support system, playing a central role in the water cycle as well as providing nutritious seafood.

With the heat of the Sun, water evaporates from the ocean's surface. The vapors cool as they rise into the sky, turning back into water to form clouds. These clouds bring rain, which is vital for our drinking water and when growing fresh food.

Create Your Own Mini Water Cycle Experiment

1. Fill a reusable ziplock bag with a little water.

2. Add blue food coloring to create a mini "sea" in your bag. Make sure the bag is firmly closed.

3. Take it to the beach with you on a sunny day.

4. Hang up the bag or pin to the top of a stick. Leave it for a few hours in the sun.

5. Check the bag for condensation. Water droplets will have formed on the inside of the bag and will be slowly falling back into the blue water, like rainfall.

6. Notice that the droplets are clear. Food coloring is heavier than water and doesn't evaporate, similar to salt in the ocean.

7. Take your bag home!

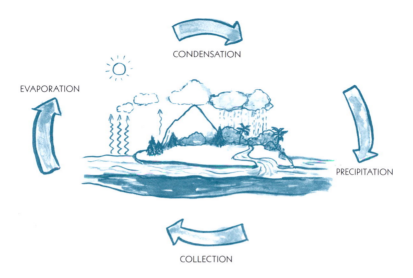

CONDENSATION

EVAPORATION

PRECIPITATION

COLLECTION

Food from the ocean also gives us important vitamins and is rich in omega-3 fatty acids, which we can't produce for ourselves. Fish represent 17 percent of our global animal protein intake, and more than three billion people depend on marine and coastal biodiversity for their livelihoods.

Unfortunately, unsustainable fishing practices have led to overfishing and habitat destruction, with 80 percent of the world's fish stocks severely depleted or on the brink of collapsing. Top predators who help keep the ocean's ecosystem in balance, like tuna and sharks, are in dramatic decline, with other species on the brink of extinction. Pollution is also a big problem for our oceans. Plastics, heavy metals, and chemicals that end up in the food chain pose a risk to human health in addition to marine life.

It is essential that we buy and consume sustainably caught seafood from local, low-impact fisheries (see page 128), avoid single-use plastics, and recycle waste responsibly.

6

Understand Climate Control

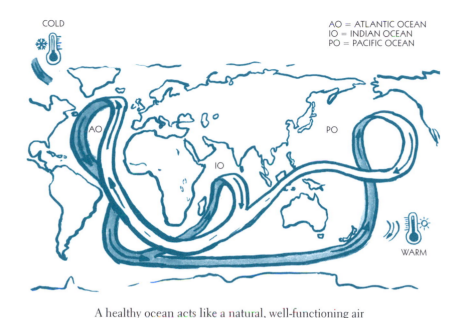

COLD

AO = ATLANTIC OCEAN
IO = INDIAN OCEAN
PO = PACIFIC OCEAN

AO

PO

IO

WARM

A healthy ocean acts like a natural, well-functioning air conditioning system for the planet and helps regulate the temperature and weather in the Earth's atmosphere. Water currents circulate the Earth, distributing the heat that the ocean absorbs from the Sun around the globe. By mixing the extreme temperatures of the poles and the equator, the ocean currents help make most of the Earth habitable. While the ocean protects us by absorbing excess heat from greenhouse gases, sea surface temperatures are rising rapidly, causing the polar ice sheets to melt and sea levels to rise. The ocean has absorbed so much carbon dioxide from the atmosphere that it has become more acidic, dissolving the bodies of shelled sea creatures and destroying coral reefs.

Reducing your carbon footprint is one of the best things you can do for the ocean. Consider switching to a green energy provider, shopping locally, and planting trees to help offset climate change. See pages 124–141 for more actions you can take.

7

Just Breathe

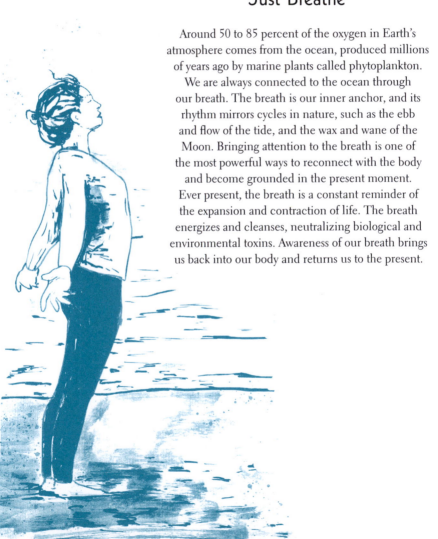

Around 50 to 85 percent of the oxygen in Earth's atmosphere comes from the ocean, produced millions of years ago by marine plants called phytoplankton. We are always connected to the ocean through our breath. The breath is our inner anchor, and its rhythm mirrors cycles in nature, such as the ebb and flow of the tide, and the wax and wane of the Moon. Bringing attention to the breath is one of the most powerful ways to reconnect with the body and become grounded in the present moment. Ever present, the breath is a constant reminder of the expansion and contraction of life. The breath energizes and cleanses, neutralizing biological and environmental toxins. Awareness of our breath brings us back into our body and returns us to the present.

A Breathing Exercise to Try by the Ocean

1. Bring your attention to your breath. Simply notice how the breath feels without trying to change your breathing pattern.

2. Consciously breathe in from your belly through the nose to a count of four.

3. Gently pause between the inhale and exhale.

4. Breathe out from the belly through the nose to a count of six.

5. Repeat, taking ten deep, gentle breaths from the belly, or until you feel just right...

If your attention wanders, gently bring your awareness back to your breath.

• FASCINATING FACT •

A type of phytoplankton called *Prochlorococcus* is so small that it can fit inside of a drop of water. In certain areas, there can be more than 100,000 cells in a milliliter of ocean water. Despite its tiny size, the phytoplankton releases countless tons of oxygen into the atmosphere. Marine biologist Dr. Sylvia Earle estimated that *Prochlorococcus* provides the oxygen for one in every five breaths we take.

8

Storm Protection

OPEN WATER   REEF CREST   REEF FLAT   SHORELINE

It has never been more important to restore marine habitats that can help protect coastal communities from the worst effects of climate change, such as increased storms and coastal flooding.

In addition to providing protection from storms and flooding, coastal habitats such as marshes, wetlands, and mangroves can absorb up to five times more carbon per acre than terrestrial forests.

Coral reefs are the most biodiverse ecosystems on the planet, supporting a rich and complex mix of life. Coral reefs protect low-lying islands and coastal shores from storms, flooding, and erosion by reducing wave energy and wave height, which in turn decreases the impact of potential storm damage on land. Unfortunately, we risk losing 90 percent of coral reefs by 2050 unless urgent action is taken to reduce global warming. We should be protecting these living ecosystems as they are our greatest allies in tackling climate change.

Notice Your Inner Weather Pattern

Sometimes it can feel as if the weather mirrors our thoughts. Some days our thoughts and feelings might feel like a storm inside of us. Just as coastal habitat restoration can protect us from storms, inner restoration can help improve our internal weather patterns. My favorite way to take care when I am by the ocean is the "Sit Spot" (see page 100).

9

Medicines from the Sea

Many solutions to human illnesses come from the ocean. Thousands of compounds from marine organisms that have been discovered help us treat diseases. For instance, a compound from a deepwater sponge was found to have potent anti-cancer properties and was used in the first anti-leukemia drug, while chemicals produced by a type of algae are used to help treat cystic fibrosis.

Other compounds are used as diagnostic tools in medicine or aid in the development of viral diseases such as COVID-19. A green fluorescent protein from jellyfish is helping scientists advance the study of the nervous system. Mussels secrete a strong sticky substance, known as "nature's glue," which helps them stick to rocky reefs in the sea. This has inspired the development of an adhesive that is being tested for use in surgery to help heal wounds. The venom from cone snails is also currently being used in research, helping treat serious medical conditions such as epilepsy and multiple sclerosis.

Unfortunately, many of these species and their habitats are at risk of extinction. We may lose many cures for diseases and viruses before they are even discovered if the destruction of marine ecosystems continues, especially in the deep ocean.

Next time you go for a walk by the sea, see how many creatures and plants with medicinal properties you can identify, such as sea sponges, jellyfish, mussels, and seaweed.

10

Sustainable Seaweed Foraging

Seaweed is an important nourishing food source found all over the world. It has been harvested for as long as humans have lived by the ocean.

Seaweeds are packed full of minerals, vitamins, and antioxidants with many health benefits, such as supporting healthy functioning of the thyroid and immune system.

There is no seaweed that is unsafe to eat; however, you may find some tastier than others. Don't worry about identifying every type of seaweed. Start with a couple you can easily recognize and get familiar with them first. Here are some of my favorite varieties to get you started.

Dulse (or dillisk) is reddish brown in color and can be eaten raw, dried, or cooked. Its salty, nutty flavor is a great addition to soups and stews, or sprinkled on salad as a salt alternative.

Carrageen grows in the Atlantic waters around Ireland and Europe and means "little rock" in Irish. It is bushy, fan-shaped, and reddish in color and can serve as a natural thickening agent (an alternative to gelatin). My grandmother used to make a delicious jelly from carrageen, dissolved in milk with honey and lemon. She also used this as a remedy for colds.

Sea Spaghetti is a dark green-brown seaweed exposed on rocky shores at low tide. It looks like spaghetti and has a similar texture. I like to use it as an alternative to pasta, letting it simmer in hot water for ten minutes.

It is incredible to watch the color of seaweed transform when placed in hot water, often turning bright green. This can help soften tougher seaweeds although all seaweed can be eaten raw. Dried seaweed will return to its natural tender state as soon as it is immersed in water again.

The only risk is contamination from poor water quality. Remember to never forage for seaweed near a stream, river, marina, stagnant water, or where there are large amounts of algal bloom, which can indicate pollution from industrial or agricultural practices.

It is very important to harvest seaweed sustainably. Never pull seaweed from the rocks. Trim no more than one third of the plant with scissors. Never over-harvest, and only take what you will use. Seaweed is so flavorful you only need small amounts.

The best time to harvest is during the spring tides, although extra caution is needed as these tides rush back in quickly, so check the tide times for your area. Never go alone, and always seek local advice if you are new to the area. Take care on the rocks—they can be very slippery!

We Are Ocean

We experience and comprehend the world through our senses. The ocean and coasts are dynamic, offering very different multi-sensory experiences to land-based environments, with important benefits for our health.

Multi-sensory environments engage a variety of our senses all at once, stimulating the brain and aiding memory. At the beach, essential high functioning sensory systems in the brain are improved, such as listening (the mix of seabirds calling and crashing waves), and tactile recognition (the feeling of sand beneath our bare feet).

The color, movement, and smell of the ocean all have an effect on our sense of well-being. The stimulation of all of these senses help us fully experience the world around us and more vividly recall these experiences, which is why early memories of water are some of our most powerful. And this is before we even dip a toe into the sea.

11

Water Bodies: The Sea Inside Us

Just as the ocean makes up 70 percent of the Earth's surface, the adult human body is approximately 60 to 70 percent salt water. Our blood is mostly water, containing a concentration of salt and other ions that is very similar to that of seawater, which further suggests our link to the origin of life in the ancient sea. After observing improvements in his patients with cystic fibrosis who surfed, respiratory physician Peter Bye discovered that inhaling salt water helped rehydrate the lining of airways and could be used as a new therapy in the treatment of the disease.

What Does Salty Water Do?

Salt water helps the body communicate by creating electrical signals that carry messages between the brain and the rest of the body. These electrical signals also power your heart.

In the same way that salt water acts as a conveyor belt of heat in the ocean to transport important nutrients and regulate Earth's surface temperature (see page 32), salt water in the human body helps regulate many functions including body temperature.

The salt in our bodies also helps us maintain fluid levels. When we get too hot, we sweat, eliminating some salt water from the body and running the risk of becoming dehydrated. This is why it's very important on a hot day by the ocean to drink lots of water to keep our water levels up. If we've been exercising and sweating, it can be a good idea to have an isotonic drink (with added salt or electrolytes) to help the body rehydrate more quickly.

Our bodies must have balance in order to thrive. Consuming too much salt in our diet can raise blood pressure, which can cause serious problems for vital organs, especially the heart.

Make Your Own Healthy Isotonic Drink

- 1 cup of herbal tea
- ¼–½ teaspoon of sea salt
- 1 teaspoon of magnesium (for added minerals)
- ¼ cup of natural fruit juice (not from concentrate)
- 1 tablespoon of natural sweetener, such as honey

1. Mix together.
2. Store in the fridge to cool.
3. Enjoy after a hot day at the beach!

12

Look at the Sea

It is no surprise that some of the greatest artists and writers throughout human history have been drawn to the ocean for inspiration. The sea is visually stimulating with a thousand shades of blue that are constantly changing.

The famous early twentieth-century writer Virginia Woolf wrote, "Each wave of the sea has a different light, just as the beauty of who we love." Modern advances in psychology and neuroscience have caught up with what Woolf perceptively captured in her writing: how just looking at the sea allows us to reflect on our well-being.

The color blue is associated with feelings of calm and creativity. According to clinical psychologist Richard Shuster, watching the ocean alters the frequency of our brain waves and places us in a more meditative state. This is especially important in a time when stress and anxiety are on the rise.

How Many Shades of Blue Do You See?

1. Next time you go to the coast, bring a sketchbook, and coloring pencils or paints.

2. Look at the sea as a color palette. How many shades of blue are visible?

3. Notice how these colors might change or blend into each other depending on the weather.

4. Paint a color chart in your sketchbook of all the shades of blue you can see.

5. Repeat this exercise on different days and seasons to compare. You may also want to note the weather conditions on each day.

Over time, you will begin to notice patterns of color and seasonal changes that reflect the different "moods" of the ocean.

Listen to the Sea

Listening to the ocean can be an antidote to the daily noises and stressors we experience in more urban areas. The richness of the sounds of the sea, like the rhythmic pulse of breaking waves, has a soothing effect on our minds. Washing over us like a "sound bath," sea sounds have the opposite effect of the unexpected staccato of traffic and other artificial street sounds that can create stress in the body.

The sounds of the sea have a measurable effect on human health and well-being, bringing a sense of calm and reducing stress. In an increasingly noisy world, listening to the sounds of the sea for just a few minutes can cause stress hormones like cortisol to drop. This can have a restorative effect for people who are ill or recovering from illness by helping to reduce tension and perceived pain in the body.

The sound of waves, gently breaking and washing onto the beach before retreating back into the ocean, helps to stimulate our parasympathetic nervous system. When activated, the parasympathetic nervous system helps us to relax and slow down, creating a meditative sense of calm.

When you go to the beach, record sounds of the sea to play when you are back at home—playing this on a loop can be a great way to soothe your nervous system when trying to fall asleep at night. Try to record the sounds of the sea at different times of the day or on different days. Can you hear differences in sound on a calm day versus a wild day?

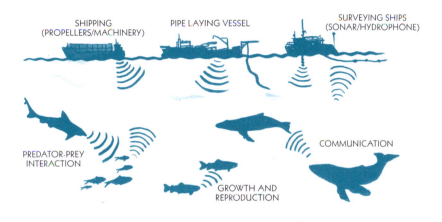

Ocean Noise Pollution

Sound travels four to five times faster in water than in air, so you can hear wider array of frequencies underwater—and the oceans are getting louder.

Noise pollution from increased shipping, seabed mining, and testing for offshore energy exploration are so loud that almost no part of the ocean remains free from noise caused by human activity. This is believed to have a direct impact on the communication and behavior of marine life, from tiny zooplankton to cod fish that can sing, to migratory whales and dolphins, which are very social creatures that are heavily reliant on acoustic communication.

For sea life, it's like living in a permanent construction zone. The good news is that when noise pollution decreases, marine habitats and sea life can recover quickly.

More Ocean Senses: Smell, Taste, Touch

Our sense of smell, taste, and touch provide strong sensations that remain deeply connected to the information they're associated with. For instance, the smell of the sea breeze sharpens our taste buds. While we are constantly exposed to positive ions emitted from our electronic devices, ocean waves release negative ions (which occur when there is moving water), and help mitigate our ion balance when we are by the sea. Negative ions are believed to alter our biochemistry and improve our mood, relieving stress. Evidence suggests that exposure to these ions could help to treat symptoms of seasonal affective disorder.

Touching sand also greatly benefits our sensory systems. Playing in sand is especially beneficial for children because it helps develop motor skills associated with tactile learning (being able to sense the world through touch and identifying changes in temperature and texture). It's not surprising how much children like to play in sand, and we should all play in the sand more throughout the course of our lives.

Group Activity: The Power of Touch

1. Collect some objects you find along the shore, combining natural and man-made objects, such as beach pebbles (a mix of smooth and rough), empty sea shells, feathers, seaweed, a bottle cap, or a piece of rope.

2. Arrange these objects in a small pile.

3. Invite your friend(s) to close their eyes or put on a blindfold and sit them next to the pile of small objects. Make sure the objects remain out of sight until they are blindfolded.

4. Ask them to describe each item using only touch. What can texture can tell us? For instance, what does the smoothness of a beach pebble reveal?

15

Mammalian Dive Response

Like dolphins and seals (our mammalian cousins),
we too have evolutionary aquatic markers.

When we are in the water, our mammalian dive response causes
our heart rate to slow, calming our fight or flight response.
This is called bradycardia (the medical term for "heart slowing"),
and is triggered when our face first comes into contact with water.
Nerve receptors in our face respond to the sensation of water
by helping prepare our bodies to hold our breath so that we
can dive underwater.

The mammalian dive response activates what free-diving champion and founder of the I Am Water foundation, Hanli Prinsloo, calls our "inner seal," and triggers a number of physiological responses in the body. These changes allow us to relax when in water, and include diverting oxygen from extremities to essential organs (like the heart and brain), and the "spleen effect," in which the spleen releases more oxygen-filled red blood cells into the body. Our bodies remember our connection to the ancient sea from which all life evolved and the beginnings of our own lives in our mother's womb.

Tips to Connect with Your Body and Breath in the Ocean

On a calm day, enter the water and focus on your breath. When you are about knee deep, lower yourself into the water and lie back (you can gently rest on your arms if you are not comfortable floating). Let your body relax by taking a slow, deep breath in. Notice how your lungs expand, like a balloon inflating, causing your body to feel a little lighter. Gently exhale and notice how your body begins to sink a little into the water. With each breath, allow your body to soften and be held by the ocean.

To become more comfortable with putting your face underwater, take a breath in and as you breathe out, lower yourself into the water so your nose is just touching the water's surface, blowing bubbles as you exhale. After you get used to the sensation of water on your face, lower your face so that the water just covers your ears. Notice the difference in sound. Life below the surface has its own unique soundscape, and sound travels much faster underwater (see page 49).

The Power of the Sea to Heal

The deterioration of our global ecosystems is mirrored by the decline of our physical health and well-being. How do we improve mental and physical health through interactions with water? In this chapter, I share examples of the many health benefits that come from interactions with the sea, as well as cross-cultural ocean therapy initiatives that foster personal wellness and ocean awareness.

16

Self-Care Through Blue Care

Water has been celebrated for its therapeutic qualities for
thousands of years, with Taoist Lao Tzu writing in the sixth
century BC:

"Nothing in the world is softer than water.
But for attacking the hard, the unyielding, it has no equal."

In the nineteenth century, seaside holidays were recommended
by physicians for respite and recovery from illness. In indigenous
Polynesian culture, surfing is considered to be spiritually
cleansing in addition to being a sport.

Today, Western science is beginning to catch up. Evidence
shows that spending time by the ocean has a positive effect
on mental health and promotes physical activity. A large-scale
study looking at the effects of proximity to the coast in the
UK found that mental health benefits were greater for people
from poorer households, suggesting that coastal settings may
help reduce health inequalities. A global review of activities in
and around water found that the sea is the most studied water
environment for healing.

Journal Exercise: How Does the Ocean Take Care?

1. Next time you're at the beach, notice what draws your attention. Maybe it's a starfish in a rock pool, seaweed along the shore, or a seabird in flight.

2. Observe whatever you're looking at in detail by noticing its behavior and how it interacts with its environment.

3. In a notebook, write some responses to questions about how this part of nature takes care of itself. What other organisms does it rely on? How does it support other life?

4. Now think about how you take care of yourself, writing these thoughts down. What do you do to nourish yourself? Who relies on you? How do others support you? What might you learn from this sea creature or element of nature that can help you take better care of yourself?

Scientist and professor of environmental biology Robin Wall Kimmerer considers paying attention to nature in this way to be "a form of reciprocity with the living world, receiving the gifts with open eyes and open heart."

17

Soothe Your Mind

We learned in pages 46–53 that the multi-sensory nature of the ocean can help soothe our minds. The sounds of the sea, blue color of the water, and negative ions released by breaking waves all help us find calm.

Given the fact that the human brain is 80 percent water, water directly affects the brain. Research shows that being near water can have a positive impact on our mental state while reinforcing our connection to ourselves, one another, and nature.

Marine biologist Wallace J. Nichols describes this human–water connection as "blue mind" in his book of the same name. *Blue Mind* explores why we are drawn to water and why it has such a calming effect on us. Nichols calls this the antidote to "red mind," which is characterized by an anxious, overstimulated, and distracted state of mind that defines much of our modern lives.

This blue mind connection helps us relax and quiet the noise in our heads, creating a greater sense of clarity. This clarity can aid reflective thinking, allowing us to take a look at the bigger picture and gain insights into our actions and experiences without judgement.

Neuroscience is beginning to highlight the relationship between water and our brain. For example, the vagus nerve is stimulated when we are in water. This nerve plays a central role in the parasympathetic nervous system, calming our fight or flight response.

The constantly changing and multi-sensory nature of the ocean is also linked to enhancing neuroplasticity, or the brain's ability to form new neural connections in response to new experiences or changes in environment. This offers novel ways to improve learning and treat physical injury and mental illness.

Take a "Blue Mind" Moment

If you can't access the ocean, evidence shows that simply looking at a picture or hearing the sounds of the sea can calm our minds. If you take a photo or make a sound recording next time you are by the sea, activate your blue mind by practicing the simple breathing exercise (see page 35), while looking or listening to your recorded "seascape." This way, you can return to your blue mind state at any moment to cultivate a sense of calm.

18

Calm Your Heart

Harbor porpoises can consciously control their heart rate to match their dive time underwater. In an increasingly stressed out society, it is important we actively try to lower heart rate. Although we can't control our heart like porpoises, we can take actions to help regulate it by consciously controlling our breath. As we learned on page 52, our heart rate slows when we are immersed in water, especially in preparation for holding our breath and diving underwater.

It's not just the sensation of seawater on our bodies but the sounds of the sea that has an effect on our hearts. The gentle pulse of the ocean mimics the rhythmic pulse of our own heartbeat. This soft, calming sound, combined with other sensory stimuli from the ocean, is believed to help lower heart rate and blood pressure. Evidence suggests that it is even possible for your heart rate to synchronize with the "rhythm" of the sea.

One of my favorite things to do by the ocean is to search for heart-shaped stones and beach pebbles as a reminder of how much the sea has to give. Next time you are at the beach, see if you can find one. The ocean has a way of reminding us of the importance to connect with our hearts, not just our heads.

19

Ocean Therapy

Organizations are tapping into the restorative power of the ocean to tackle issues like mental health and to help reverse the trend of declining nature experiences by fostering a greater emotional connection with the ocean. Research in this area is only beginning to show why being in or by the ocean is beneficial for our health.

SNORKELING
SAFARI

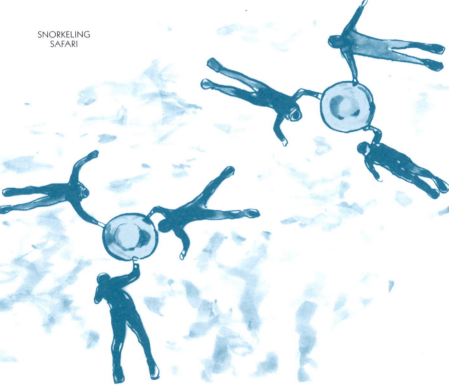

Why Is the Ocean So Therapeutic?

The unique properties of the ocean play a key role in enhancing health and wellness. For example, the absence of gravity in salt water can alter bodily sensations and improve mobility, as well as heart and lung function. The weightlessness also provides an important muscular workout, especially for people with disabilities.

Being immersed in water can offer a sense of freedom from earthly limits, as one participant in an ocean therapy study described: "Diving turns me back into a human being. I go down there and I've got the freedom and I'm back to being a person."

Findings from a global review suggest that challenge can be an important factor for sustainable well-being and self-worth. Different coasts, winds, currents, and seasons require constant adaptation, as we respond to nature in the moment.

The last five years have seen a rapid increase in the use of surfing as therapy for vulnerable populations. A global review of "blue care" activities found surfing to be one of the most studied pastimes.

Other beneficial ocean therapy activities include sailing, swimming, kayaking, snorkeling, snorkeling safaris (participants are guided by a marine expert and have a life ring for support), diving, beach walks, exploring rock pools, and simply sitting by the ocean.

- Before going to the beach, write down how you are feeling.

- While you are by the sea, or during an activity like snorkeling or swimming, notice what feeling is most alive within you and make a note of it.

- On your return, record how you are feeling now.

- Reflect on your list of feelings. Did you notice any changes? Were there particular elements of the experience that influenced how you felt at the beach?

20

Be Like Water:
Creating Connection

In Iran, surfing emerged as a sport when it was first introduced by women in 2013. Although this activity was initiated by women, the challenge for women to access these experiences persists.

I founded Be Like Water with Shirin Gerami, Iran's first female triathlete, in 2015 as a way to make surfing more accessible to women and girls and to facilitate a greater body–self–nature connection. By first connecting with our breath and bodies, we become more self-aware and confident in the water. Taking this new understanding into the surf, through "wave play" (see page 120), we learn how to tap into the power of waves in a playful way that builds trust in our bodies and in the ocean. As a result, we connect more deeply with those around us and become more alive to our environment.

In Gerami's words, wave play allows us to "celebrate the beauty in our differences through the playfulness of the sea and surfing." My experience with women in the Be Like Water program has taught me that the ocean does not discriminate and fosters deep connections.

We all have our own way of moving. In Iran, women have to cover their bodies by law, yet getting more in touch with how our bodies feel in the water is such a universal experience that it transcends cultural customs. That, for me, is what's most important, making this experience as accessible as possible.

21

Liquid Therapy

There has been a steady increase in the use of surfing as therapy for vulnerable and diverse groups to promote psychological, physical, and social well-being.

Liquid Therapy was created in Ireland in 2011 to provide support for young people who want to experience surfing but are unable to participate in mainstream opportunities.

Founder Tom Losey believes that "Surfing is the tool, the mechanism to create change, but it's not the outcome. It's not about learning to surf; surfing is simply the vehicle that enables this process of change."

Liquid Therapy provides a fun, safe environment and offers surfers the opportunity to grow and flourish. Their surf and ocean therapy activities encourage personal development—from social interaction to balance and coordination.

Surfing involves active engagement and immersion in the ocean, providing a sense of respite from anxieties and disabilities. Research supports the benefits of surf therapy that include an increase in self-esteem and confidence for young people. For example, feelings of stress and anxiety before surfing are replaced with greater feelings of happiness.

The health benefits of surf therapy are linked to the fluid and dynamic nature of surfing and the sea. The feeling of waves breaking over the body and the sensation of water pressure on the body can enhance feelings of well-being. Learning to surf in a group context can also help promote a sense of belonging and identity through shared experiences in the surf.

Learn to Surf

Why not give surfing a go? Enroll in a surf school next time you go to a surfing beach. Notice the dynamic energy of the waves and how your body's response to balancing on the board is a workout for the entire body. The feeling of catching your first wave—being pushed to the shore by the power of nature—feels like flying. You may experience a buzz of adrenaline and an increase in endorphins, which surfers refer to as "stoke."

Flower Power by the Sea

Plants that grow by the sea are extremely resilient, having adapted
to a harsh, salty, and rapidly changing environment. Most plants
and flowers have evolved with unique adaptations and are specific
to a particular coastal habitat, meaning they don't grow anywhere
else. Sea sandwort has white, star-shaped flowers and grows on
beaches and sand dunes. The flower's thick fleshy leaves help lock
moisture in and its deep root system can withstand salty winds
and shifting sands.

My favorite flowers are sea thrifts, also known as sea pinks. To me, they symbolize resilience, growing in clumps of poor soil on the edges of cliff faces and rocky crags. In early summer, bright pink flowering globes like lollipops burst atop tall, thin stalks. Sea pinks have adapted to life in harsh conditions and are at times even submerged by the sea. They use the salt water to protect their leaves and can survive on very little water.

Being creative outdoors by making art promotes well-being. Explore the seaside by looking for flowers and plants unique to the area, sketching your favorites. Notice what shapes, colors, and textures you are drawn to. You could zoom in and draw the detail you see in the pattern of the leaf, or zoom out and draw the flower in its surrounding habitat. Instead of sketching or drawing, you could make a rubbing of a leaf, or if a flower has been broken in the wind, make a pressing.

Note: Coastal habitats are very vulnerable to outside disturbances. Do not pick flowers found by the sea! They may be a rare species and are happier providing pollen for pollinators like bees.

The Sea is Calling

Once discovered, the call of the ocean can be hard to resist.
People have been drawn to the ocean for centuries, not only
to fish and forage for food, or to travel and transport goods,
but also to relax and play. The rhythm of the sea calls upon
us to tune into our own rhythm and relax. The wide open
blue horizon invites us to pay attention to the world around
us in a different way. A sandy beach can offer a wonderful
canvas for the artist in all of us. In this chapter, you will learn
how to deepen your connection with the ocean in a playful
and responsible way.

23

Beachcombing

Beachcombing consists of searching for found items along the shore, such as seashells or driftwood. This pastime likely originated during a time in which our human ancestors gathered food or driftwood for fuel and were made curious by unfamiliar objects. Beachcombing can help support conservation and research. By noticing changes along your local coast, you may be the first to identify a pollution incident, or alert the relevant organization to help save a stranded marine animal. Beachcombing is also an activity that can be done in tandem with beach cleaning activities (see pages 133–136).

I like to think of beachcombing as trying to decipher the ocean's story through the objects it casts ashore. Recently, an increasing number of items found along the shore tell a sad story of wasteful human habits.

The ocean also teaches us about currents when it transports tropical seeds, or "sea beans," to shore. Sea beans can be different shapes and sizes, and are believed to hold magical properties, especially for women trying to conceive. Some sea beans have been passed down from mother to child for generations.

Occasionally, long-buried objects are revealed, such as a whale tooth from the eighteenth century, when whalers hunted whales for their oil to power streetlamps.

Beachcombing is an incredibly meditative way to pay attention to the natural world. Look carefully for objects like beach pebbles with a unique pattern, unusual pieces of driftwood, "mermaids' tears" (sea glass), or a "mermaid's purse" (an empty egg case capsule). Remember, shells are vital to marine ecosystems. Please don't take them away from the beach!

24

Shark Conservation and Egg Case Hunting

Beachcombers make great citizen scientists. By contributing
to surveys like the Marine Biological Association's Sealife
Survey, you can share what you saw, where you saw it and when.
Another citizen science initiative is the Shark Trust's Great
Eggcase Hunt, a global survey which records the discovery of
the hatched eggs of sharks and skates (a type of ray) in order to
identify species presence and diversity around the world.

All skates and some sharks reproduce by laying eggs. After
the eggs hatch, the egg case, a leathery capsule known as a
"mermaid's purse," washes ashore.

The size, shape, and color of the case can help scientists identify
which species it belonged to and learn more about the behavior
and migratory patterns of sharks and skates.

There are surveys happening around the world—register your
own "egg case hunt" and contribute to the conservation of these
important species.

Why Is It Important to Protect Sharks and Skates?

Sharks are apex predators, which means they support a healthy, resilient ecosystem by helping regulate species abundance. The presence of sharks is a key indicator of ocean health, and many shark species are under severe threat. One hundred million sharks are killed every year, many of which are caught illegally for their fins. Skates are heavily fished, and under similar threat as sharks, yet receive very little conservation attention.

Egg Case Hunting Tips from the Shark Trust

- Be safe on the beach. Check the forecast and tide schedule, keep away from the base of cliffs, and use a stick to search through seaweed.

- Respect wildlife and habitats. Do not take live animals from the seashore.

- Egg cases are usually found in seaweed on a tide line. They can blend in really well so keep an eye out.

- While egg cases can be found year-round, the seaweed and debris that washes ashore after a storm provides a prime egg case hunting ground.

- Check to make sure the egg case is definitely empty. Empty egg cases have no secondary purpose—they don't provide a home for hermit crabs and will not break down to form sand.

- When you find an empty egg case, take a photo and record your findings on Shark Trust's global database or your local conservation survey website (see page 143).

25

Discovering Seashells

Seashells are the hard, protective outer layer, or exoskeleton, created by many marine animals. These shell dwellers are typically mollusks, such as sea snails, and bivalves, like clams and oysters. It is estimated that the number of known shell-dwelling species ranges from 70,000–120,000.

Shells are made from calcium carbonate produced from the skin of the mollusk's body. A shell found along the beach could be days or thousands of years old. Shells are one of nature's most remarkable designs. Here are a few patterns to look out for.

The spiral design of many shells appears throughout nature—in sunflowers, hurricanes, and in constellations. Whorl patterns are believed to symbolize creation, infinity, and the cyclical nature of life. Throughout human history, the sacred geometry of shells has inspired art and architecture. Shells have long been admired by humans and used as adornment, currency, and in spiritual ceremonies throughout the ages.

The conch shell in particular holds special meaning in many spiritual traditions, including Islam, in which it represents hearing the divine word, and Buddhism, in which it represents awakening from ignorance. It also holds important meaning in Hinduism, Christianity, and many indigenous cultures. Conch shells are known around the world to be use as trumpets, with the earliest found trumpet dating from 6000–3000 BC. In Polynesian tradition, this type of instrument, otherwise known as a "pū," has been used in ceremonies since ancient times. Today, conch shells are still used in special ceremonies, including weddings, and at sunset to give thanks for the day.

In ancient China and India, cowrie shells were used as money. Traders introduced the cowrie currency to Africa where it gradually spread to many places around the globe, remaining in circulation until the mid-twentieth century. Cowries were also valued as charms for healing, fertility, magic powers, or good luck. In ancient Greece, the cowrie shell was referred to as "kteis," the same word used for scallop and vulva.

Given the beauty and value of seashells, it may be tempting to collect the shells you find, however this can be harmful for the ecosystem and the species that rely on them for survival. For example, hermit crabs rely on empty spiral shells for their home and protection. Since hermit crabs can't make their own shells, they must find an empty one to dwell in. As the hermit crab grows, it needs to find a larger shell to live in, and will die if it can't find the right shell.

Other marine animals, such as the octopus, will often hide behind empty shells to avoid predators. Some species will even use discarded or broken shells as building material. Seaweeds and corals attach to shells in order to stay on the seabed. Some shells are even collectors themselves—the carrier shell attaches smaller empty shells to its surface to increase its size, adding shell "spikes" for protection.

With an increase in beach tourism and people taking shells from the shore, beach erosion and biodiversity decline are becoming more prevalent. Instead, why not take pictures of the shells you discover and create a photo album? You can use a seashell pocket guidebook or download a shell identification app to help you identify the shells you discover (see pages 142–143).

Important: It is illegal to buy or sell seashells. Shells for sale as souvenirs have most likely come from a living animal that was killed for the purpose of selling. Never collect seashells with living creatures still in them. Not only will the creature die if removed from the sea but some shells are extremely poisonous. For instance, the cone shell's venom can be deadly.

26

Explore a Rock Pool

Exploring tidal rock pools is one of my favorite childhood
memories. At an early age, I learned about the vibrant habitat of
intertidal zones from time spent exploring rock pools.

When to Explore

Timing is essential when studying rock pools. It's best done in warmer, calmer months during low tide. The rock pools closest to the sea are home to the most sea life.

What to Spot

Seaweeds, anemones, crabs, shrimp, starfish, urchins, and all sorts of fish and sea snails…

Some of My Favorite Things to See

My favorite fish to spot is the blenny, a fish that likes to hang out on the bottom of the pool while resting on its front fins. If you are very still, and careful not to splash or cast a shadow, you may be able to spot a blenny fish pumping water through its gills.

Limpets, a type of sea snail, are a very common sight around the edges of rock pools on any shore, but that doesn't make them any less fascinating. They have incredible suction which makes them almost impossible to remove from practically anything. The teeth of a limpet are the strongest biological material tested in the world and are stronger than Kevlar (the material used to make bulletproof vests). They are able to withstand the same pressure required to turn carbon into diamonds. This incredible discovery could help advance many technological innovations, from the automotive industry to dentistry.

Many starfish live in rock pools and are amazing animals to discover. They don't like to be taken out of water, so if you decide to handle a starfish, please do so in the pool. Starfish will let you know if they are becoming stressed by curling the tips of their arms up—a sign you should put them down.

Sea anemones are often the most colorful sea life in rock pools. While they could be mistaken for a plant, sea anemones are actually a predatory animal that anchors itself to the bottom or sides of a pool. With red, purple, or pink tentacles, their swaying limbs entice small sea creatures that end up getting caught in the anemone's stinging tentacles. Amazingly, sea anemones can cheat

death by constantly replacing their bodies with new cells, enabling them to stay young. Although most anemones cannot harm us, as our skin is coated in oils and bacteria, our touch can cause them serious harm.

Spend time observing and getting to know the sea creatures you discover in rock pools. What are they telling you about themselves? How do they interact with other creatures and their environment?

• THE SEASHORE CODE •

o **Stay safe**—pay close attention to the returning tide. Allow plenty of time to leave before the tide reaches you, or you may suddenly find yourself cut off from the shore.

o **Show respect for all sea life**—leave seaweed in place and carefully replace any stone exactly as you found it.

o **Take photos home, not animals**—try to avoid handling any creatures and always return them to their rock pool homes.

o **Watch where you step**—walk carefully to avoid causing damage to plants and animals, or slipping on seaweed. Slip-resistant footwear is recommended.

27

Jelly Watch

Scientific research institutes need your help monitoring jellyfish. By sharing your observations, scientists can build a global database, helping us better understand what is happening in our oceans.

Why is Jellyfish Data Important?

Jellyfish have been part of the marine ecosystem for 500 million years and are an important part of the marine food web. Dramatic increases and shifts in jellyfish "blooms," or large swarms of jellyfish, have been reported around the world, and scientists are trying to understand why. This phenomenon is believed to be linked to warming sea temperatures and lower oxygen levels in the sea caused by climate change and pollution.

Great examples of citizen scientist initiatives are the Jellywatch in the United States, the Big Jellyfish Hunt in Ireland, and the Great British Jellywatch Weekend in the UK. These projects are asking for your help in providing information about jellyfish you observe when you are by the sea (e.g., the color and size, if dead or alive, or if it was part of a bloom, etc.).

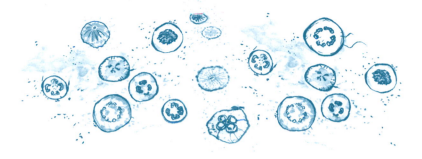

Next time you are by the ocean, look out for jellyfish. The best time to spot them along the tide line is after a warm day, windy weather, or heavy rain. Finding jellyfish on the beach is usually a sign that there are jellyfish in the water. It's best not to touch any jellyfish in case they sting. Instead, consider taking a photo and report your findings (see page 143).

• WHAT TO DO IF YOU GET STUNG BY A JELLYFISH •

Some jellyfish have very small stinging cells in their tentacles called *nematocysts*. While their tentacles are used to capture prey for food, a jellyfish will sting if you brush up against them.

1. Remove any tentacles from the skin with tweezers.
2. Rinse the area with vinegar.
3. Immerse the injured area in hot water, or apply a hot compress.
4. Rest to keep inflammation down and stop the sting from spreading.

If, in very rare cases, the symptoms worsen or a severe reaction occurs, seek medical help immediately.

28

Seaside Scavenger Hunt

This is a game my parents used to play with my sister and me, turning the beach into a magical treasure hunt full of incredible things to be found.

A scavenger hunt is a fun activity to do with friends or family. Make a list of things to find by the ocean or at the beach, take a bucket to collect the items, and go hunt!

Ideas For Your Scavenger Hunt:

- something old

- something new

- a hatched shark egg
  (a "mermaid's purse")

- sea glass ("mermaids' tears")

- a stone with a hole in it

- a crab shell

- something with a spiral pattern

- something blue

- something that feels smooth

- something that feels rough

- something slippery

- something that tickles.

Share and discuss your treasures—it's exciting to see the many
different ways we interpret the same idea.

29

Sand Art

Sand is an amazing medium to use for sculpting, from building miniature sandcastles with a bucket and spade, to incredible, larger-than-life sand sculptures. The longest sea sculpture measured just under seventeen miles (27.3 km) long, and broke the Guinness World Record. It was built in 2011 on Schaabe beach in Germany with the help of 11,000 volunteers!

There are hundreds of sand sculpture festivals all over the world featuring competitions for sand artists.

Sand Art Challenge

Once you master the simple sand castle—filling a bucket with damp sand, packing it tightly, and turning the bucket upside down to reveal your creation—organize your own sand art competition with your friends and family for fun or as a fundraiser for a good cause.

Try to sculpt a mermaid, seabird, jellyfish, or surfboard out of sand. Beachcomb first to gather natural and man-made objects that could be used to embellish your design, such as seaweed for a mermaid's hair or tentacles for a jellyfish, and seashells or bottle caps for eyes. Be sure to take away any ocean litter you find and dispose of responsibly.

Another simple and fun way to create sand art is to use the beach as your canvas. With a garden rake or stick, draw patterns and images in the sand. Celebrate the beauty of impermanence by letting the incoming tide erase and reclaim the beach.

The sea also creates its own sand art. After it rains, visit the beach to see beautiful patterns made by the water as it tries to find its way through the sand and back to the ocean. Depending on how much wave action there is on a calmer day, the sea may leave behind perfectly formed ridges or ripples that contour the beach. Taking photos or sketching these patterns can be great inspiration for the artist in all of us.

30

Sand Boat Building

My favorite childhood activity was to head to the beach with my little sister and build a sand boat. We'd then climb into our boat and wait for the incoming tide to reach us so we could "set sail." A thrilling battle with the tide followed, in which the sea always won. As the waves reached our "boats," we frantically and hopelessly tried to bail out the water. The game was to see which one of us could hold out the longest before getting completely soaked by the sea and having to "abandon ship."

How to Build a Sand Boat

1. Using a stick or your fingers, draw the outline for your boat in the sand.

2. Along these lines, dig out a deep moat and pile up the sand to build the sides of your boat. If the sand is very fine or crumbly, use a little water to make it easier to sculpt and shape.

3. Add some features to the interior of the boat like a seat by using stones or sand.

4. Finish off by adding shells for control buttons and pieces of driftwood for a sail and rudder.

5. If you want the sea to reach your boat so you can "set sail" faster, dig a channel from the water's edge to the moat around your boat. As the tide comes in, your moat will fill with water.

31

Beach Mandala

A mandala is an ancient art form, often representing a spiritual connection with the world. Dating back to early human history in the spirals and concentric circles found in rock art, the mandela is considered to represent the cycle of life. Today, it is found throughout cultures and used in art therapy.

The beach offers the perfect canvas to express your creativity. Creating a beach mandala is one way to represent the cycles connected with the ocean — the waves, the tides, and the Moon. After beachcombing, create a personal or group mandala using found objects.

Begin by standing at the center of what will become your mandala, drawing a small circle around yourself with a stick. Then draw a bigger circle outside this one, and repeat as many times as you like.

When creating a mandala as a group, you may want to take turns adding shapes, objects, or patterns until the mandala is complete.

This form of creative play is an essential way for us to explore, learn, and adapt to our environment, no matter what stage of life we are at.

32

Fly a Kite

The simple joy of kite flying has been around for two to three thousand years, and a wide open beach is the perfect place to learn to fly a kite or perfect your skills. All you need is a gentle breeze and a partner to launch the kite up into the air. Make your own kite to take to the beach with these simple materials.

What You'll Need

Two sticks or wooden dowels — one approx. 47 in. (120 cm) for the spine, and the other 35 in. (90 cm) for the crosspiece

Recycled plastic bag or a sheet of newspaper

Scissors

Pencil

String

Tape

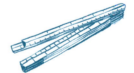

Ruler

Twine

Ribbons

How to Make Your Kite

1. Lay the longer stick vertically (this will be the spine of your kite).

2. Locate and mark with a pencil the middle point of the crosspiece.

3. Roughly 12 in. (30 cm) from one end of the spine, place the crosspiece so its midpoint intersects with the spine at a 90-degree angle.

4. Fasten the two sticks together tightly with twine and tape, making sure they remain perpendicular.

5. Run twine around one end of the crosspiece before wrapping it around all four points of the kite and fastening at each point using tape.

6. Lay out your plastic bag or sheet of newspaper, placing the frame on top with the crosspiece facing up toward you.

7. Cut out the shape of your kite, leaving about 4 in. (10 cm) outside of the frame.

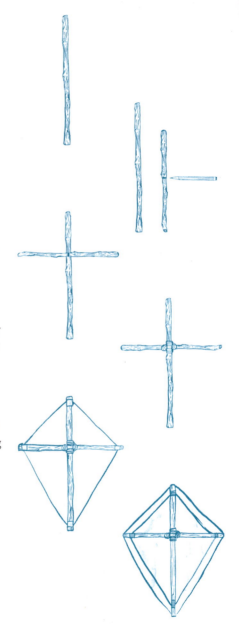

8. Fold the extra material over the frame and secure with tape.

9. Using a pencil, carefully punch two small holes, one near the top and one at the bottom end of the spine, for the bridle (the string that will attach the kite to the flying line). Reinforce these holes with tape.

10. Feed the ends of a length of twine through both holes, securing two knots around the top and bottom of the spine. When you pick up the kite by the bridle, there should be at least 8 in. (20 cm) between that point and the kite's surface.

11. Near the top of the kite, attach the flying line to the bridle. Where you attach the string controls the angle at which the kite flies, so this made need some adjustment when you test it at the beach.

12. Attach a length of string to the bottom end of the spine as a tail to help stabilize the kite. Tie ribbons to the tail at regular intervals (if you don't have ribbon, use leftover plastic).

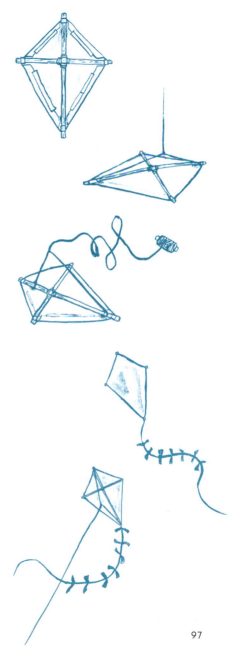

33

Relax and Restore

It's little wonder why we are drawn to the beach as a place to relax. As we learned on pages 48 and 59, being by the ocean soothes our nervous system and can help trigger the release of serotonin, the hormone that plays a key role in boosting our mood.

In our busy lives, simply "doing nothing" may feel like a luxury or an impossible task. Some of us may even equate doing nothing with being unproductive. However, doing nothing is important for our creativity, and being by the ocean can be the best place to "do" just that!

Task Yourself with Doing Nothing

Next time you go to the beach, try doing nothing for a while. Sit or lie still on the beach without focusing on anything at all for ten minutes. Let any thoughts or feelings that arise wash over you like a wave breaking on the sand before disappearing into the sea. Don't try to analyze or judge any of your thoughts. If you find yourself getting too distracted or reaching for your phone, try the Sit Spot or Sound Mapping exercises (pages 100–105) to help you tune into the present.

In today's world, we suffer from information overload. When the mind and body get a chance to rest, our imagination sparks, allowing us to discover new insights and be inspired by the ocean.

34

Sit Spot

Being still by yourself in nature can have a calming and restorative effect. One way to connect with the sea is by creating a place, or "sit spot," where you can be by yourself and observe the sea through your senses—the rush of the wind across the water, the sound of waves crashing, and the feeling of the sun or wind on your skin.

Your "sit spot" is where you can let go of your thoughts. This works best if you can find a special place you can visit regularly so you can build a more intimate connection by noticing patterns and changes through the seasons. This practice can leave you with a profound sense of awe and gratitude.

Pick a quiet place by the sea.
Go there a lot. Just sit, relax, and
breathe it all in.

This meditation works well
combined with the
sound mapping
exercise on page 102.

35

Sound Mapping

Sound mapping is a great way to slow down and cultivate a greater awareness of our surroundings in minutes. It is especially effective when the surf is up and lovely to do with friends and family.

How to Sound Map

1. Go to the beach and find your "sit spot," a safe space where you will not be disturbed.

2. Get comfortable. You may even want to lie down and close your eyes.

3. To heighten your sense of hearing, try cupping your hands behind your ears.

4. Listen for sounds that are nearby and far away, high-pitched and low-pitched.

5. Notice what is making different sounds—seabirds, wind, waves, other people.

6. If there are waves breaking, can you try to pick out the "sound signature" of a particular wave? Is there any pattern to the sounds of breaking waves, or is it chaotic? Can you hear a quieter "lull" between breaking waves?

7. For the last few moments, try not to focus on any specific sound at all. Let the mix of sounds wash over you like a symphony.

8. Before you move, you might like to draw a "map" of the sounds on the sand. Keep it simple, marking your position with an "X" in the middle, maybe drawing wavy lines to symbolize the sounds of the waves or birds, for example.

9. Notice how you feel after this practice.

10. Share your experience. What sounds were familiar? What sound had you not noticed before? Which sound did you like best?

• WHY DO YOU HEAR THE OCEAN WHEN YOU PUT A SEASHELL UP TO YOUR EAR? •

Although it does sound a lot like the ocean, the sound you hear when you "listen" to a seashell is not actually the sound of the sea but ambient noise, or the combination of sounds all around us. The round, curved surface of a shell is great for reflecting sound. Because every shell is a different shape and size, the sound you hear from each shell is unique, amplifying ambient noise and different frequencies. Remember: before picking up a shell and putting it to your ear, make sure there are no sea creatures living inside!

Don't forget to bring the benefits of listening to the sea into your everyday life. Play a recording of the ocean's soundscape to aid relaxation and focus (see page 59). This is also a simple, yet powerful, exercise that can be shared with those who are visually impaired.

36

Have an Eco-friendly Picnic

Having a picnic by the ocean is a beautiful way to enjoy the outdoors. Unfortunately, our food habits can create a bit of a mess and negatively impact our environment, especially the sea. Please avoid single-use plastics (now banned in some parts of the world including the Hawaiian Islands and the European Union), and replace them with eco-friendly alternatives.

Tips For an Eco-friendly Picnic

- Prepare a homemade meal to take with you. Rather than buying pre-packaged food that is less fresh and likely wrapped in plastic, try to buy local and organic produce.

- Prepare finger foods that don't require cutlery.

- Bring drinks in reusable water bottles.

- Try out compostable plates made from natural or recycled materials.

- Bamboo utensils are a great plastic alternative—they're reusable, biodegradable, and more durable than plastic.

- Pack food in reusable containers or wrap with beeswax wrap (a great alternative to plastic wrap).

- Seek out some shade with a beach umbrella or a wide-brimmed sun hat.

- Bring a picnic blanket to sit back, relax and enjoy your time by the ocean!

- Leave your picnic area better than you found it. Take home all leftovers and dispose of any trash. Better yet, incorporate a quick beach clean into your post-picnic activities (see page 134).

37

Seabird Watching

Seabirds have been around for sixty million years and have adapted to living by, on, and in the ocean. There are about 350 species of seabirds and many are known for undertaking great migrations—the longest is the Arctic tern's migration from the Arctic to the Antarctic! Seabirds are either coastal, meaning they spend most of their time out at sea, or land-based, spending long periods of time away from the ocean.

Seabirds have adapted to their ocean habitat in some incredible ways and most have waterproof plumage. One exception is the cormorant, which you can spot with black feathers and a bright yellow beak standing on rocks with its wings spread out to dry. Gannets are excellent divers, plunging into the sea at speeds of up to 62 mph (100 km/h) to catch their prey.

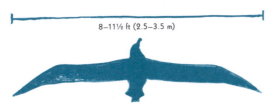

8–11½ ft (2.5–3.5 m)

The largest seabird is the wandering albatross, with a typical
wingspan ranging from 8–11½ ft (2.5–3.5 m). Their ability
to glide while in flight allows the birds to travel incredible
distances, clocking around 75,000 miles (120,000 km) a year.
The smallest seabird is the storm petrel at a size of 4½–10
in. (12–25 cm). The petrel spends most of its life at sea, only
coming ashore to breed. Both birds form lifelong bonds with
their mates and can live for over thirty years!

Seabirds are recognized for their key role in guiding fishers to
shoals of fish and early explorers to land. However, colonies of
seabirds have been wiped out by hunting, with entire species at
risk of extinction—including the much-loved puffin, known as
the clown of the sea for its colorful beak. Seabird populations
around the world are in serious decline as a result of human-
driven factors, including overfishing, habitat destruction,
climate change, toxic pollution, and ocean plastic. Seabirds
are important indicators of ocean health—when seabirds are
hurting, the ocean is hurting too.

Seabird watching can be a wonderful spectacle, especially witnessing their aerial acrobatics high above sea cliffs and expert fishing skills diving for fish. Remember that you are a visitor to their home and to be respectful.

Seabird Watching Tips

• Do your homework. Research the seabird species common to your local beach and how to identify them.

• Prepare for bad weather with suitable clothing and footwear.

• Stay safe. When possible, remain on designated paths and keep back from cliff edges or the base of cliffs.

• Do not feed the seabirds.

• Seabirds are vulnerable to human disturbance, especially during breeding and nesting seasons, so watch at a distance. Remember to take your binoculars.

• Mind where you step, some seabirds nest on the ground, such as plovers, terns, and sandpipers.

• Contribute to their conservation. Record observations in the BirdLife's International Seabird Tracking Database, one of the biggest marine conservation collaborations in the world, with millions of recorded observations.

• An estimated 90 percent of seabirds have ingested some form of plastic, and as a result, one million seabirds die every year. Support initiatives to ban single-use plastics in your town or country and enforce stricter penalties for polluters.

• Support seabird conservation charities. For more ways to help protect seabirds and marine ecosystems, see pages 124–141.

38

Whale and Dolphin Watching

A world without whales would mean an ocean without song. This loss would also likely bring about the collapse of marine food webs, and the effects of climate change would worsen, as whales help reduce the amount of carbon dioxide in the atmosphere.

Whales were hunted almost to extinction until commercial whaling was banned in 1986. The current population is estimated to be 1.3 million, one quarter of the population pre-commercial whaling when over four million whales swam the oceans. Fifteen species are endangered, while some are dangerously close to extinction, like the blue whale. Unfortunately, Iceland, Norway, and Japan still carry out commercial and "scientific" whaling. Whales also face an array of threats from other human pressures like pollution, rising sea temperatures, and fatal collisions due to increased global shipping.

Whales and dolphins are marine mammals, classified as cetaceans, which have evolved over fifty million years. Blue whales are the largest animals ever known to have lived on Earth at 82 ft (25 m) long and can live to be nearly 100 years old. While all dolphins have teeth, only some whales do, such as beaked and sperm whales. Many whales have keratin bristles, known as baleen, instead of teeth that they use to filter food like crustaceans and small fish from the water. Whales can dive very deep—the deepest whale dive ever recorded was by a Cuvier's beaked whale, diving almost two miles (3 km).

• FASCINATING FACTS •

Whales and dolphins are highly intelligent and social creatures with their own distinct languages. These marine mammals communicate by using a complex mix of sounds that can travel hundreds of miles underwater, some of which create a pattern of sound that is similar to a human song. Each species and individual family has their own language or "song," and are able to alter their song when meeting other cetaceans.

Whale pump is a term used to describe the important role whales play in the ocean by recycling nutrients and enhancing marine productivity. Since whales dive into the depths to feed, their waste brings nutrients from the deep water to the surface. This waste promotes the growth of phytoplankton—a key player in the food web—and reduces the impact of climate change by absorbing carbon dioxide.

How to Spot Whales

Whales are migratory and can be seen from the shore at certain times of year. To spot them, look out for a plume of spray jetting up into the air that signifies a whale has surfaced to breathe. Some whales, such as the humpback, will show their tail, or "fluke," above the surface when diving down into the ocean. Recorded sightings of a whale displaying its tail helps scientists identify individual whales, as each whale has a unique tail shape, like a human fingerprint.

Tips for Responsible Whale and Dolphin Watching

• Find a tour operator that prioritizes conservation, supports the local community, and follows best practices, such as those outlined by the World Cetacean Alliance. This includes approaching whales slowly and sideways; never getting too close; reducing speed when whales are spotted; and limiting the number of vessels in a single area at any one time.

• A responsible whale and dolphin watching trip will have an expert guide on board.

• Watching on land is inexpensive and much less invasive. In the Azores islands in the mid-Atlantic, special lookout towers, or "vigias," once used to look for whaling boats, are now used for whale watching.

The gold standard for sustainable whale and dolphin watching destinations are Whale Heritage Sites. Established by the World Cetacean Alliance, Whale Heritage Sites are locations where people and cetaceans coexist in an authentic and respectful way.

Look for Bioluminescence

I first discovered bioluminescence at dusk while paddling a kayak in Lough Hyne, a marine nature reserve on the southern coast of Ireland. As I dipped my paddle into the briny water, a glowing swirl of light sparkled and lit up the dark like an underwater galaxy. It felt magical and otherworldly, like paddling through an ocean of stars.

Bioluminescence is light produced and emitted by living organisms. While this can also occur in terrestrial species like fireflies, this phenomenon is widespread among marine species such as jellyfish, plankton, and bacteria. Bioluminescent creatures can be found across the world from deep ocean to shallow coastal waters.

Bioluminescence is believed to serve as a form of communication that some species may use to attract mates, repel predators, or hunt for food.

This seemingly magical light is produced by a chemical reaction in the organism's body caused by luciferin, a molecule that reacts with oxygen to produce light. Dinoflagellates, a type of plankton that lives on the surface of the sea, respond to changes in natural light causing them to glow after sunset. They can be spotted as a sparkly sheen when waves break onto the shore.

While bioluminescent algae is rare, there are some coastlines around the world where blooms appear more frequently, so research any local sightings before visiting the coast. The best time to spot bioluminescence is usually during the summer months, with little moonlight when the tide is coming in, although visibility is not guaranteed. The water needs to be disturbed in order for the bioluminescence to light up, which is why you can spot it more easily when there are breaking waves.

Bioluminescence additionally has many uses in medicine and can help detect diseases in the body, leading to improved diagnoses. It can also help treat neurological disorders by illuminating electrical impulses in the brain.

40

Walk Barefoot

Evidence shows that when we are by the ocean, we are more likely to be physically active. While walking is good for us, walking barefoot along the beach is even better.

The foot has around 200,000 sensory receptors which can provide us with a wealth of feedback about our environment. Unfortunately, these receptors are rarely stimulated as we spend so much time indoors or wearing shoes.

The Benefits of Walking in the Sand

• As we walk on the beach, the shifting sands require extra effort on our part to balance the body, gently working our muscles.

• Going barefoot on the beach stimulates the sensory receptors in our feet, strengthening the sensory feedback between the feet and brain. This helps our bodies better "read" the ground and our brains become more responsive and adaptive.

• This sensory stimulation helps us feel more grounded, energized, and reconnected to the natural world. In traditional Chinese medicine, stimulating certain areas of the foot helps to release or balance energy in the body.

• Letting children go barefoot on the beach is highly beneficial for their development and helps them establish a healthy relationship between their bodies and nature.

• Bringing our awareness to the texture and movement of the sand beneath our feet also helps us become more present in the moment and less distracted by our thoughts.

41

Wave Play

Also known as bodysurfing, wave play means to ride or float on
the crest of incoming waves without using a board.

When I want to shift my perspective or I am struggling
with a creative block, I jump into the sea. Wave play allows me
to just be. I surrender myself to the power of the waves, feeling
the energy of something so powerful lift and move my body. I
learn to go with the ocean's flow.

Let's Move Like Waves!

1. Read the sections on risks and safety before you begin (pages 18–27). Pick a day when the waves are around 1–3 ft (less than 1 m) high.

2. Wade into the shallow waters no further than the waist-high.

3. Notice what happens when you meet an incoming wave with force. Brace yourself like a football player and tense your body for impact as the wave comes toward you.

4. Slowly come to the surface, gently rising up. Become aware of your surroundings.

5. As the next wave approaches, focus on your breath, allow your body to soften, and the wave will carry you to shore.

6. Notice the difference between these two wave encounters. How did it feel to surrender to the wave instead of resisting?

• IMPORTANT SAFETY INFORMATION •

Observe the conditions before jumping into the ocean. Keep to the shallows and be aware of changes in the tide and current. Find your bearings by determining two fixed points on land to stay in line with. Before entering the water at a place you are unfamiliar with, learn about the local conditions from lifeguards or experienced water users. Rip currents (see page 24) and *undertow* can be dangerous, sweeping even the most powerful swimmers away in an instant.

42

Sea Swimming

Swimming in the sea requires us to focus on the breath, calming our anxieties and aiding relaxation. When I joined the sea swimming group Ebb and Flow on the West coast of Ireland, they shared their philosophy of "relax, let go, flow."

Ebb and Flow encourages swimmers to focus on the sensation of movement, not distance or speed. This mind–body–place connection can help turn a potentially risky and unpredictable environment like the ocean into an empowering one.

First, bring an awareness to the body, consciously breathing to help relax and let go of tension, which aids an easier, smoother swimming stroke.

Swimming in cold water (59°F/15°C or less) can feel especially invigorating because our skin holds three times more cold receptors than warm. This stimulates the vagus nerve in the brain, lowering cortisol and releasing feel-good hormones like dopamine.

Even being immersed in cold water for as little as one minute increases electrical impulses in the brain and gives the body a mini workout, boosting metabolism. Gradual immersion in cold water can additionally increase the number of white blood cells in the body, strengthening the immune system to fight infection and reduce inflammation.

• IMPORTANT SAFETY INFORMATION •

Before swimming in the sea, make sure you are taking the necessary safety steps: never swim alone; swim parallel to the shore; stay in the shallows where your feet can touch the seabed; do not swim after drinking alcohol; and look out for rip currents. When possible, join a local swim group or swim at a lifeguard-patrolled beach. See page 27 for tips on embracing cold water immersion safely.

Things to Do for the Sea

Climate change experts and authors of *The Future We Choose: Surviving the Climate Crisis*, Christiana Figueres and Tom Rivett-Carnac, emphasize the importance of a mindfulness practice to help you "create a gap of light between yourself, the world, and your reactions."

How important is our role in protecting the sea? Everything we consume has an impact, with most of our waste ending up in the sea. The cumulative effect of pollutants is reducing the resilience of entire ocean ecosystems, with unpredictable and potentially disastrous consequences for both marine and human life.

Cultivating greater mindfulness allows us to become more conscious of our actions, to act as citizens and not consumers, and to spend our money on ethical and sustainably made products. Let this be one of your mantras: Reduce, reuse, recycle. This chapter presents some simple yet effective examples of mindfulness in action, such as the Think Before You Flush campaign (see page 137).

43

Be a Conservationist

The Sustainable Development Goals (SDGs) are seventeen
global goals set by the United Nations General Assembly.
Described as a "blueprint to achieve a better and more
sustainable future for all," the assembly hopes to see these
goals take shape by 2030.

The fourteenth goal, SDG 14, is called Life Below Water. This
goal aims to protect, conserve, and sustainably manage the use
of marine resources for a better future.

As we've learned, a healthy ocean is essential for
a healthy planet.

Everyone can help! Below are a few goals to create action around
to conserve and sustainably interact with the ocean:

- Reduce marine pollution.

- Conserve coastal and marine areas.

- Research ocean health and increase scientific knowledge.

- Support sustainable, small-scale fishers.

If we can't take action in our homes and at work to reach these targets
directly, spread the word about the importance of SDG 14. Petition
local government officials and corporations to take action so we can
enjoy a healthier ocean and more sustainable future.

44

Eat Sustainable Seafood

Billions of people depend on the ocean as an essential source of protein. Sustainable seafood is caught or farmed in a way that promotes long-term abundance, does not harm marine ecosystems, and supports livelihoods of fishing-dependent communities. Unfortunately, a lot of seafood is unsustainably harvested, and overfishing has lead to the collapse of fish stocks and the breakdown of marine ecosystems. It is important to choose seafood that has been harvested or caught using low-impact fishing equipment (e.g., static gear like pots that don't damage the seabed).

Here are a few tips to help you get to know your seafood and make more sustainable choices.

• Download a seafood guide like the Monterey Bay Aquarium's Seafood Watch that provides information on which types of fish have been overfished (see page 142). Choose a seafood guide that also flags which types of seafood contain levels of mercury or PCBs (polychlorinated biphenyls). These highly toxic chemicals often build up in larger fish, posing a risk to human health.

• Seafood Watch recommends you avoid the following: bluefin tuna, farmed salmon, eel, sharks, imported shrimp, and wild caviar, among others.

• As a rule of thumb, eat fish that are lower down in the food chain and rapidly reproducing, therefore recovering more quickly. Sardines and mackerel are perfect examples, both rich in omega-3 fatty acids which are vital for our brain and heart health.

• Oysters, clams, and mussels from an area with good water quality can be a sustainable option.

• Regenerative ocean farming is an innovative approach to sustainable seafood that uses the entire water column—from sea surface to seabed—to grow seaweed and shellfish. This practice not only provides us with sustainable seafood but creates more marine plant life to absorb carbon from the atmosphere.

Simple and Delicious Seafood: Steamed Mussels

Fresh mussels should smell like the sea. Discard any that smell fishy or are cracked or open before cooking. You may need to scrub the shells to remove any barnacles, algae, or "beards" (fine bristles on the edge of the shell).

1. Add a splash of water (or white wine) to a large pot over medium heat.

2. Add chopped shallots and garlic for extra flavor.

3. Place the mussels into the pot, stir to coat and increase heat to high.

4. Cover pot with a lid and steam for five minutes.

5. Once the mussels have opened, they are ready. Discard any that remain closed.

6. Serve in bowls with broth from the pot. Mop up the excess broth with hearty bread.

45

Be Sun Savvy

Every year, up to 6,000 tons of sunscreen is estimated to wash into the sea, damaging coral reef ecosystems. The chemicals in sunscreen can disrupt the coral's life cycle and cause bleaching, killing the coral.

Choose sunscreens that are mineral-based or free from harmful chemicals, especially oxybenzone and octinoxate. Hawaii became the first state to ban the sale of sunscreens with these chemicals. Scientists are gathering more evidence on other chemicals used in sunscreens that may also be harmful.

Better yet, cover your body with ultraviolet protection factor clothing (UPF), which will block the Sun's harmful rays so you don't need to apply as much sunscreen in the first place.

46

Leave No Trace

Leave No Trace is a global outdoor education initiative that recognizes our responsibility to care for and respect nature, encouraging minimal impact.

When you go to the sea, you are a visitor. The best way you can give thanks to the ocean is by making sure that you take everything you brought to the beach home with you. Leave only your footprints in the sand for the tide to claim.

You may wish to go one step further with a beach clean, leaving the beach even better than how you found it (see pages 134–136).

47

Two-Minute Beach Clean

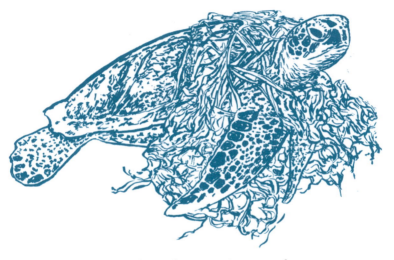

Plastics have a devastating impact on the ocean.
They are not biodegradable like organic material, instead
breaking down into smaller pieces called "microplastics" that
accumulate toxins and end up in the food chain. Plastic waste
is harmful to marine wildlife as they can become tangled in
discarded fishing nets and ropes. It can also be mistaken for
food by a wide variety of species, including turtles, whales,
seals, birds, and fish, which can die as a result. It's easy to feel
overwhelmed with some of the challenges our planet is facing,
but there are actions you can take. As co-founder of Protect Blue
Linzi Hawkin asks:

"'What difference will one plastic bottle make?'
said 7 billion people."

There are some incredible campaigns happening globally that you can be a part of. One of my favorite movements is the #2minutebeachclean, originating in the UK after a series of brutal storms in 2013 left beaches littered with marine plastics. Using Twitter and Instagram to raise awareness, Martin Dorey came up with the idea of cleaning just two minutes during each beach visit and began using the hashtag. Since then, thousands of posts using the hashtag have appeared on Instagram and Twitter from every continent.

Join the initiative by bringing gloves and a trash bag next time you visit the beach. Take care to avoid handling any dangerous or sharp objects, and dispose of garbage responsibly.

This is a great activity to do with friends and family. Use this as an opportunity to start a conversation about the items you use and could you do without. Imagine the journey of that item. Where did it come from? What did it "see" while making its way across the ocean?

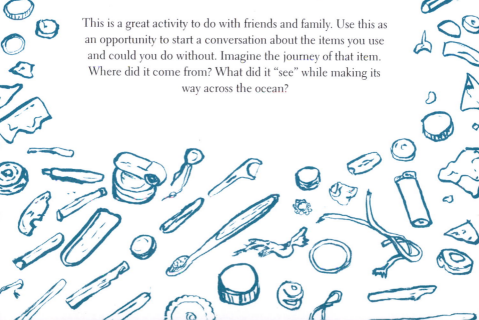

48

Take One
Small Action

Millions of marine animals become entangled and trapped by bags, plastic rings, and fishing nets. While it can sometimes feel overwhelming when confronted with the amount of marine litter on beaches, every small action makes a big difference.

Removing litter that features a loop or ring, such as the packaging used to hold drink cans together, is one such action I learned from ocean activist and artist Sabine Springer. Selectively picking up the most harmful debris could help save a marine animal's life.

This activity also brings greater awareness to the everyday items we may use and throw away without considering their impact, reminding us to reduce, reuse, recycle.

Go one step further by engaging your local government and demand they take action against these harmful practices. We can affect change if we support initiatives and raise awareness of these issues. And change is happening. For example, an eco six-pack ring for drink cans, made from compostable brewing waste, has been designed to replace harmful plastic rings.

49

Think Before You Flush

Think Before You Flush is a public awareness campaign initiated by Clean Coasts in Ireland that has since spread to other parts of the world.

Everyday items are flushed down the toilet that end up in our waterways and oceans. The biggest culprits are: baby wipes, facial wipes, cleansing pads, toilet roll tubes, Q-tips, medicines, cigarettes, band-aids, diapers, tampons, tampon applicators, and sanitary pads. These items should be disposed of in a trash can.

When possible, replace any of the items listed above that you use with eco-friendly alternatives that can be reused and will biodegrade when you dispose of them. For instance, try using a cotton cleansing cloth instead of disposable face wipes, or a reusable menstrual cup instead of tampons.

50

Restore Coastal Habitats

Marine and coastal habitats like mangroves, salt marshes, sand dunes, seagrasses, and kelp forests play a vital role in reducing the worst effects of climate change by absorbing and storing carbon dioxide from the atmosphere. They also benefit ocean and human health by providing important habitats for marine species, enhancing biodiversity, protecting food security, and helping communities adapt to climate change by offering protection from natural disasters.

Magnificent Mangroves

When we think of forests, we tend to think of land-based forests rather than those that exist in the ocean. Mangrove forests are found in the shallow warm waters of tropical seas. Their tangled root systems prevent erosion, improve water quality and clarity by filtering the water, and provide a sheltered nursery for juvenile fish. Mangroves also protect shorelines from damaging storm surges and floods. Unfortunately, half of the world's mangroves have been cleared or destroyed, and more are being lost each year due to man-made coastal development.

Restoration of mangroves is a key solution, not only in regenerating marine biodiversity and protecting seafood supplies but in tackling climate change. In addition to protecting against storms, mangroves are "carbon sinks," absorbing more carbon than rainforests.

You can support "blue" tree planting initiatives like Sea Trees, which helps fund community mangrove restoration projects. Be wary of "carbon offsetting" schemes—the amount carbon that is actually sequestered can be uncertain and offsetting can reduce the incentive to actually reduce greenhouse gas emissions. Coastal habitat restoration projects should be supported for the multiple benefits they provide.

Marvellous Marram Grass

Coastal sand dunes also protect against erosion and flooding. Dune vegetation, especially a coarse coastal plant called marram grass, plays a vital role in maintaining healthy coastal ecosystems, trapping sand to help stabilize the dune system and providing a home for highly specialized and rare species.

Walking or playing on sand dunes can damage this fragile ecosystem and exacerbate coastal erosion. Activities such as quad biking and building campfires in this environment can be extremely harmful. The good news is that damaged dunes can be restored by transplanting marram grass into eroded areas to limit the direct impact of waves. There are many examples of communities coordinating with local authorities to restore coastal ecosystems in this way.

Restoring and protecting healthy sand dunes is a natural solution to enhance biodiversity and help buffer coastal communities from the effects of climate change. Check out local coastal organizations to participate in dune restoration, or form your own group and petition local government to support marram grass planting.

Super Seaweed

While seaweed is found on coasts around the globe, consider its role underwater—forming the forests of the sea, absorbing carbon dioxide, and providing oxygen, nutrients, and habitat for hundreds of marine species. Restoring seaweed, especially macroalgae like kelp forests, can help rebuild underwater ecosystems.

Kelp provides important compounds that are found in items we use in everyday life, such as health supplements, skincare products, fetilizer or compost, and *biofuel*. Seaweed is also being used as an eco-friendly alternative to plastics.

The best thing you can do to protect ocean health and the healthy functioning of important marine and coastal habitats is to take climate action.

Identify how you can reduce your carbon footprint by at least 50 percent in the next ten years to support global emission reduction targets. When possible, travel less, carpool, ride a bike, or take public transportation. Buy lasting or eco-friendly products, support local growers, eat sustainably caught seafood, and begin the switch to 100 percent renewable electricity. Most importantly, exercise your power by engaging in politics and making climate change your number one issue.

Glossary

Biodiversity The variety of all life on Earth as well as the diversity of the communities, habitats, and ecosystems formed by plant and animal life.

Biofuel A fuel that is produced from natural, living, and/or organic material, such as seaweed. If sustainably managed, biofuels can be a source of renewable energy.

Blue Care Activities in, on, or by the sea with a therapeutic purpose, such as surf therapy.

Blue Space All visible outdoor surface waters, including rivers, lakes, and seas.

Neap tides Occur when the Sun and Moon are perpendicular to one another, causing moderate tides.

Ocean The World Ocean that covers over 70 percent of the Earth's surface area and contains 97 percent of its water. The ocean comprises five major divisions: Pacific, Atlantic, Indian, Southern (Antarctic), and Arctic.

Sandbar A long, narrow bank of sand found at river mouths, estuaries, or just off the beach where a bank or mound of sand is built up by waves. A sandbar is often exposed at low tide and may be submerged at high tide.

Sea Bodies of water much smaller than oceans that are located where the land meets the water. Seas are partially or fully enclosed by land.

Spring tides Occur during a new or full Moon, when the gravitational pulls of the Sun and Moon cause very high and low tides.

Undertow A current of water below the surface of the sea that is formed by a retreating wave.

Sources

Apps, databases, websites

Seabird Tracking Database
http://www.seabirdtracking.org
A citizen science initiative by BirdLife International in which you can contribute to the largest collection of seabird tracking data in existence.

Seafood Watch
www.seafoodwatch.org
Ocean-friendly seafood guides and sustainable seafood recipes by the Monterey Bay Aquarium to help you make better choices for a healthy ocean.

Seas, Oceans & Public Health in Europe (SOPHIE)
www.sophie2020.eu
This site provides useful reports, policy briefs, videos, and infographics to reveal the important links between ocean health and human health.

The Shell Museum App
www.shellmuseum.org

This app by the National Shell Museum helps you identify thousands of shells by using the camera on your phone. While specific to the southwest coast of Florida, many of the shells are found around the world and more are being added to the database.

Tides Near Me
www.tidesnear.me
This app helps you search for the tide times at your nearest local beach or coastal area.

The Weather Channel
www.weather.com
For information including wind speeds, swell heights, and the times for sunrise and sunset.

Further reading

The Beachcomber's Companion by Anna Marlis Burgard and Jillian Ditner

Blue Mind by Wallace J. Nichols

Braiding Sweetgrass by Robin Wall Kimmerer

Eco-Art Therapy by Theresa Sweeney

Edible Seashore by John Wright

The Future We Choose by Christiana Figueres and Tom Rivett-Carnac

Guide to Edible Seaweeds by Prannie Rhatigan

The Sea Around Us by Rachel Carson

Shells: The Clearest Recognition Guide Available by S. Peter Dance

"Undersea" by Rachel Carson

UN Sustainable Development Goals
www.un.org/sustainabledevelopment/
sustainable-development-goals

Organizations and campaigns

The 2-minute Foundation
www.beachclean.net

Black Girls Surf
www.blackgirlssurf.com

I Am Water
www.iamwaterfoundation.org

International Surf Therapy Organization
www.intlsurftherapy.org

Jellywatch
www.jellywatch.org

Leave No Trace
www.lnt.org

Liquid Therapy
www.liquidtherapy.ie

Sea Sisters
www.seasisterslk.com

Sea Trees
www.sea-trees.org

Shark Trust
www.sharktrust.org

Think Before You Flush
www.thinkbeforeyouflush.org

World Cetacean Alliance
www.worldcetaceanalliance.org

Acknowledgments

My deep and abiding gratitude to the ocean as a constant source of inspiration, well-being, and restoration in my life, and for all that it does for us.

There have been so many people in my life whose mentorship, wisdom, support, and encouragement have deepened my sea connection. A special thanks to: Prof. Michael Depledge for introducing me to the concepts of blue space and blue health; Prof. Lora Fleming and the SOPHIE team's research on Oceans and Human Health; Dr. Wallace J. Nichols and his "blue mind"; Free diver Hanli Prinsloo for sharing her underwater world; Theresa Sweeney whose nature therapy work inspired the "Self-Care through Blue Care" activity in this book (see page 56); and Dr. Ayana Elizabeth Johnson's leadership on climate and ocean policy.

I'm especially grateful to all those who have helped restore and celebrate the ocean as a safe and healing space, especially Martina and the Sea Sisters team, the female surfers of Iran, and the Liquid Therapy family.

To the amazing team of women at Pavilion who helped make this book possible—in particular, Lucy, Alice, Cara, and Izzy: I thank you. A special thanks to Krissy Mallett for her support, encouragement, and incredibly helpful suggestions that have helped give this book its flow. Artist Maria Nilsson has been a joy to collaborate with—it's been a pleasure to see her bring the text to life with her beautiful illustrations.

I'm forever grateful to my parents for fostering such a deep and abiding love for the sea in me and my sister from the moment we were born, and for teaching us many of the playful and creative activities found in this book.